MY MEMOIRS OF THE
DARK SHADOWS
CONVENTIONS

From August 1993 – June 2016

AuthorHouse™
1663 Liberty Drive
Bloomington, IN 47403
www.authorhouse.com
Phone: 833-262-8899

Because of the dynamic nature of the Internet, any web addresses or links contained in this book may have changed
since publication and may no longer be valid. The views expressed in this work are solely those of the author and do
not necessarily reflect the views of the publisher, and the publisher hereby disclaims any responsibility for them.

Any people depicted in stock imagery provided by Getty Images are models,
and such images are being used for illustrative purposes only.
Certain stock imagery © Getty Images.

This book is printed on acid-free paper.

ISBN: 978-1-6655-2503-9 (sc)
ISBN: 978-1-6655-2504-6 (e)

Print information available on the last page.

Published by AuthorHouse 05/12/2021

authorHOUSE®

CONTENTS

INTRODUCTION

When I was staying in New York City during the 1980's, I use to purchase some Dark Shadows' videos on VHS Cassette tapes. I remembered the serial a little from my childhood during the very, very late 1960's into the early part of the 1970's, which is the decade that the serial went off the air. However, at the time that I watched Dark Shadows on television at the time I specified, I did not consider Dark Shadows to be a serial; I thought Of Dark Shadows as a scary show which actually frighten and enticed people to watch at that time.

It premiered late in the afternoon; one character in particular interested me was Lara Parker who was a sexy, beautiful, blonde woman who had the most adorable and unusual green eyes that I ever laid on a white woman. Lara Parker's character was not good; she portrayed a witch, but no one would actually believe it, because Of her outstanding beauty. As a child watching Dark Shadows, I did not have the experience of life nor the IQ at that time to fully.

I understand the show's concept. I basically understood the Vampires, Witches, Ghosts, Werewolves, Zombies, Phoenixes, and Warlocks; and any other creatures of the Supernatural. The witch was portrayed by Lara Parker. The name given to the witch was Angelique. The Supernatural aspects of Dark Shadows is what I truly enjoyed.

The sight of a Vampire seething his or her teeth into a victim's neck was frightening. The vampire was actually making a withdrawal of Blood from the victim. What was so surprising about the vampire, He or she would go to the same victim until all the blood is Withdrawn from the system or find a new victim and continue the same process as with the other victim.

The sight of a witch sticking a pin into a doll causing a person to have chest pains or a heart attack thrilled and amazed me at that time. The witch would also cast a spell using a personal item from the Individual whom the curse will be placed. With its theme and eerie soundtrack, Dark Shadows amazed fans all around the world at that time, and to this present day.

Because of this phenomenal serial with it's special effects to emphasis

The Supernatural, Dark Shadows remains a favorite for generations and

Generations. It was this phenomenal serial which sparked the

Dark Shadows Convention during the 1980's to be held on the

Westside of the United States, and then a year later, on the Eastside of

The United States. I did not start to attend the Conventions until the

1990's.

CHAPTER ONE

New York, New York 1993: While watching an episode of Dark Shadows on VHS tape, I saw and heard an advertisement about a convention That was schedule to be held at the Marriot Hotel in New York City. At that time, I did not know the convention was connected to the Dark Shadow's serial that used to aired during the 1960's. I made a Reservation for one day at the Dark Shadows Convention during the Month of August in the year 1993 at the Marriott Hotel on 1535 Broadway, New York City, New York 10036. I was quite amazed of the attendance at the convention; but after all, it was a convention

Many members of the cast were present from the 1966-1971 serial Presentation. I thank God to this day, and I was able to see Ms. Lara Parker in person; if you examine my previous notations, you will understand that fact. Just for the record, the following actors, and Actresses were present in 1993:

Louis Edmonds, Kathryn Leigh Scott, Roger Davis, Marie Wallace, Micheal Stroka, Donna Wandrey, Paula Laurence, and Alex Stevens. The most important actor of all-the late Jonathan Frid. The 1993 Convention was huge and exciting. There was a great crowd of people to support the remaining cast of Dark Shadows.

I enjoyed this convention, because everything was on schedule. The speakers, actors, and actresses. Video highlights from various Episodes of the Dark Shadows' serial were shown. It brought back Some memories when I use to watch it on television. The next Most exciting part of the convention was seeing the Sellers and Merchants of the various items for sale which were influence from The Dark Shadows' serial. The Merchants and Sellers were stationed in Gigantic conference rooms which housed an abundance of Souvenirs such as pictures of the stars, posters, soundtrack to the Serial, video cassettes, and DVD's of the Dark Shadow's shows; there Were also jewelry, books, t-shirts, sweatshirts, and a variety of items For sale. One factor I enjoyed about the Dark Shadow's convention was the attendees were from various walks of life; Most were rich, and from The Caucasian race.

Men, Women and children attended the conventions, and sometimes, it would seem like family. In my personal opinion, what made the Dark Shadows' conventions so special, the Original cast members made themselves available to the public and their fans concerning their careers on Dark Shadows, and gave us some tidbits pertaining to some parts of their private and personal lives. In the middle of the aisle, a microphone was situated for the attendees of the convention to ask questions from the guest speakers. Many a persons would line up single-file to ask his or her own Question from the guest panel. It was educational and fun to hear the various questions from the attendees to the guest(s) on the panel. At the moment, I can not recall a specific question that caught my Attention at the 1993 convention.

At the conclusion of the convention, it was common practice to get a Signature from the guest(s) on the panel. I was fortunate to get exactly seven signatures from the original cast members of the serial. That particular experience was exciting, and I made up my mind, at the Time, that I wanted to attend another convention when it is held on the East side.

CHAPTER TWO

The Dark Shadows Festival Convention was in New York City during the Month of August, in the year 1995. At the time, I was very excited to attend another convention pertaining to this phenomenal soap opera. I attended the convention for one day. The convention was similar to the convention of 1993; however, they had different cast members to attend the ceremony; I managed to get the signatures of those cast Members, and they are as follows: Kathryn Leigh Scott, Roger Davis, Christopher Pennock, Diana Millay, Michael Stroka, Denise Nickerson and Sharon Smyth. It was a learning experience as I explained earlier to Learn about the cast members' history, and their individual views concerning their participation in working on the set of Dark Shadows. Amongst the cast members, each member was a fan of another cast Member. One actor would comment on another's actor performance on the serial Dark Shadows. It was like going back in time (My time, Childhood days of the late 1960's and early 1970's.)

Like at the previous convention, the Vendors were present to sell various souvenirs from the serial, and the merchandise that was actually made from that time period. It was exciting to see Dark Shadows' cards, pictures, pens, figurines, soundtrack albums, T-shirts, coffee mugs, etc. etc. My only regret about the Dark Shadows'

Convention that I possessed at this time in 1995, I could not afford to travel to

the west coast to participate in the Dark Shadow's Convention when it was held

on the Westside of the United States. I had to wait until the convention was held

on the eastside of the United States; otherwise, it was fun and exciting!

CHAPTER THREE

The Year is now 2001, and this is my third attendance at the Dark Shadows Convention held at the Marriott World Trade Center, New York, NY 10048. This convention is special, because it marks the 35th year that Dark Shadows-the serial has premiered on television, and been in syndication since 1966. To get to this hotel in New York City, I did not have to travel far. The hotel was located in downtown Manhattan; However, I believe everyone knows the horrific and terrible fate that happened to the World Trade Center, and the Thousands and thousands of people who lost their lives on September 11, 2001 when the United States of America was viciously attacked by terrorists who received their just punishment. I always informed people that I was at the World Trade Center Approximately three weeks before the terrorists' attacks on that Building and other parts of the United States. Enough said of that Sad, and evil day in the United States, let's get back to the Dark Shadows Convention of 2001.

The Convention was like the other two conventions with the exception that a Special Tribute was made to the actors and actresses who Played on the Gothic Serial, and died over the years. It should be noted that Louis Edmonds (1924-2001) passed just a couple of weeks before the 35th Anniversary of Dark Shadows. As with the previous Dark Shadows' conventions, at the end of the convention day, at that Time, it was customary that the dais guests would sign the attendees' Program books with their signatures. I received the autographs of David Selby, John Karlen, Roger Davis, Marie Wallace, Christopher Pennock, and Donna Wandrey. I often thought, if these Programs from the conventions, along with those autographs, would the programs be worth money; if that be the case, what will be the Value? In conclusion, the convention that celebrated the 35th Anniversary of the serial Dark Shadows being on the air, Provided a special section in ***Remembrance" for the past actors and actresses who went to that City of Gold; Their names are as follows:*** Grayson Hall, Joan Bennett, Joel Crothers, Thayer David, and Robert Gerringer.

It should be noted that these actors are my favored, and at this Moment as I write this memoir, I would like to make a personal Comment on each actor, and how his or her performance on Dark Shadow's influenced my performing skills.

Ms. Grayson Hall portrayed different characters when Dark Shadows Ran on television for five years. I will never forget her portrayal of Dr. Hoffman who discovered that Barnabas Collins was not human, But part of the living dead; he was a vampire. Dr. Hoffman learned That Barnabas was cursed by a witch in his previous life. Dr. Hoffman pledged her loyalty to Barnabas Collins that she would find a cure for his curse as a vampire. She explained to Barnabas How she can perform certain procedures to change his blood pattern which would prevent him to get an *urge* to take a bite out of someone in order to survive. Indeed, I could not imagine no other Actress to portray Dr. Hoffman than Grayson Hall.

The next actress to discuss will be Joan Bennett. She, indeed, was Beautiful and graceful. Like Grayson Hall, Joan Bennett had many roles On Dark Shadows. I enjoyed the role of Elizabeth, the Matriarch of The Collins Family in modern times;

She kept her remaining family together after her husband disappeared; Elizabeth was in charge of Collinwood estate, not her brother, Roger, nor her daughter-Carolyn. I enjoyed Joan Bennett's role as Naomi, the mother of Barnabas during the 1797 Flashback segment.

Dark Shadows always had a tendency to go back in time to Discover how someone was cursed, and how that person came to existence during present day Collinwood. It was during the 1797 Flashback, the audience of Dark Shadows discovered how Barnabas Collins became a vampire; Barnabas Collins was portrayed by Johnathan Frid.

Joel Crothers was a very, very attractive man and an actor. His performance on Dark Shadows was short in contrast to the Actual running of the Dark Shadows Serial. Joel Crothers had many different parts on Dark Shadows; I will never forget the Part he played as Maggie Evans' boyfriend. He was caring and loving to Maggie Evans.

But what I really liked about Joel Crothers was his performance on The Soap Opera-Somerset. He was dynamite. He reminds me today when I first started out in show business. Young, attractive, mustache, and hair well groomed, I received a lot of work pertaining to show Business. Somerset was a Soap Opera that premiered when I was in junior high school, and maybe high school. It was a great Soap Opera, because Joel was paired with a beautiful actress to love and make love; however, that Soap Opera was short lived.

Thayer David had many roles also in Dark Shadows; I am very fond of His role as Professor Stokes; Professor Stokes was over whelm with His theories concerning parallel time. A theory that there are two Universes that run together and each person has another counterpart; however, the lives are different, because in each universe, the Individual made a choice that influence his or her life to be different indefinitely. Professor Stokes' theory helped Barnabas through The serial to help find a cure for that curse.

Actor Robert Gerringer was an actor who was on the first popular Episodes of Dark Shadows after Johnathan Frid made his debut on the Serial. Robert Gerringer played Dr. Woodard who went to medical School with Dr. Hoffman. Dr. Woodard would come to know Barnabas' secret like Dr. Hoffman. Unfortunately, Dr. Woodard would be killed and taken off the serial. These are some of my personal Tidbits concerning those actors and actresses that I believed crossed The River Jordan and are now in that city of gold.

CHAPTER FOUR

The year is 2004, and Dark Shadows Convention is being held at the Westchester Marriott Hotel located in Tarrytown, New York 10591. Unfortunately, due to the incident at the World Trade Center in 2001, The Dark Shadows Fan Club was forced to find a new location for its convention in the Tri-State area of New York City. Tarrytown Is located forty-five minutes from the island of Manhattan if you use Metro Train from Grand Central Station to the town of Tarrytown. I enjoyed my train ride on Metro-North, because it allowed me to Leave the city on the weekend, and get a different view of the New York City Area altogether. Tarrytown is located somewhat Upstate New York, and the scenery is gorgeous.

When I arrived at the hotel in Tarrytown, I was an attendant as A Trustee at Cornerstone Baptist Church located in Brooklyn, New York. I enjoyed the convention as always.

The Convention was similar to the other three conventions that I Attended. I did not get in line to get signatures from the guests; being that I was someone of importance at that time when I was a member Of the Board of Trustees at my church. Handling the Church's finances, and property is no joke. It requires hard work and discipline. The fans of Dark Shadows were out in numerous numbers. It was a little difficult to travel to this convention because it was outside the city limits. This convention marked an important Milestone in my life. I had stature and prominence.

CHAPTER FIVE

The Year is 2006, and the location of this Dark Shadows Convention Is located at the Marriott Hotel 333 Adams Street, Brooklyn, N.Y. In this particular year, and at this particular Dark Shadows Convention, The Fortieth Anniversary of the Serial Dark Shadows was being Celebrated for being in existence. Many acknowledgements were handed out to various actors, actresses and professional people who contributed to the Serial Dark Shadow's success for the past forty Years. It was at this convention that the Creator of Dark Shadows (Dan Curtis) had passed, and gone to the city of Gold. The Convention Recognized the Late Dan Curtis' achievement concerning the Creation of Dark Shadows.

Video clips from the Serial, the Dark Shadows' movies, and Dark Shadow's Specials were all shown to celebrate the Life and Legacy of Dan Curtis who put together this marvelous Soap Opera-Dark Shadows.

CHAPTER SIX

It is the year 2007, the month of August in the city of Tarrytown, N.Y. I am attending my sixth Dark Shadows Convention at the Marriott Westchester on 670 White Plains Road. This convention marks the Fortieth anniversary of the performance of Jonathan Frid as the Vampire Barnabas Collins on the serial Dark Shadows.

As you might expect, this was a well-received audience that was very Responsive to this anniversary reception at the convention. The serial Dark Shadows was on the air for about a year when the ratings for the Serial were going down, and it looked as if the serial would be removed from channel seven line-up daytime programing.

Let's go back a little when the soap first premiered. In 1966, Dark Shadows premiered as a regular daytime serial; however, the ratings of the soap were dropping. The Creator and Producer of Dark Shadows thought of an idea to boost the ratings up for the serial and channel seven.

The Creator and Producer of Dark Shadows was Dan Curtis. Dan Curtis thought of an idea to make Dark Shadows more Popular than the other soap operas. He thought of the fact Of Ghost telling on the soap opera. As mention earlier, the soap opera starts off slow and somewhat dull. You had one, two or maybe three Main characters where the plot of the soap evolves around the three, and some background players.

Dan Curtis thought of Ghost telling because he remembered some Stories that were told to him as a child, and believe it or not, some Houses and some sound stages were thought to have been haunted. Therefore, to make the soap juicier, Ghost telling was told in More than four episodes until eventually a Ghost did appeared on Dark Shadows while using special effects to make the Ghost(s) Materialize. This worked for a while, and the ratings did go up; to make the serial more scary and spooky, Mr. Curtis added the *Phoenix-a* creature that is believed to arise from burning ashes every one hundred years.

The Phoenix in Dark Shadows was a lady who had a son name David. With the arrival of this character, the ratings went up, but not to out-number the ratings of the other soap operas. The Phoenix did some damage here and there, but not enough to make Dark Shadows that all-time classic Gothic Soap Opera.

Dan Curtis thought of another idea, the introduction of a Vampire; but this vampire will not be your typical vampire, but a more sympathetic vampire. Enters Jonathan Frid, the man of the hour at the fortieth anniversary of his celebration of being cast on Dark Shadows. Jonathan Frid was cast as Barnabas Collins, the Vampire of all time especially, on network television. When Barnabas made his debut on Dark Shadows back in 1967, the studio Executives were hopeful that this new and spooky character will boost the ratings of the serial higher than the other soap operas at that time. In fact, the introduction of Barnabas Collins as a cousin from England did boost the ratings of the show.

If you were to follow the episodes, Barnabas Collins was not actually a cousin from England; he was in fact a direct ancestor of the Present day Collins Family who lived at Collinwood.

Barnabas Collins, as you will learn, married a woman not knowing she was a practioner of Blackmagic. This storyline, of course, took Place in 1797. Back to the convention, in celebration of his Fortieth anniversary, Jonathan Frid recalled some favorite moments From Dark Shadows. Mr. Frid also conducted Dramatic Readings from his various performances. There were tons of Jonathan Frid and Dark Shadows memorabilia being sold at the convention. It was a very enjoyable evening, and one that I will never forget. By the way, it was Barnabas' spooky character, the vampire that boost the serial ratings. Jonathan Frid took his career and the serial Dark Shadows to a new and higher level. With his performance, the various storylines, and gothic features, the serial Dark Shadows Jumped its ratings on other soaps at that time, and became a

Phenomenal success of all time!

CHAPTER SEVEN

The Year is 2009, Dark Shadows Convention is being held at the Renaissance Newark Airport located in Elizabeth, New Jersey 07201. The convention was held from Aug 14-Aug 16 2009. This convention brings back sweet memories, because it was the only time that I Attended the convention for the whole three days. Generally, when I attended the convention, I would attend one day out of the Three days to show my support for the serial, and the Dark Shadows Fan Club. As always, attending the convention was rewarding and Educational. There was always something new to learn from the Convention. When I attended this convention in Elizabeth, New Jersey, Anthony Taylor completed his Trustee Stewardship at Cornerstone Baptist Church Brooklyn, New York from Jan 2001 Through Jan 2007. It was rewarding and satisfying to know that the Dark Shadows Fan Club and Conventions contributed to my success in completing my Stewardship as Trustee at my church.

CHAPTER EIGHT

The Year is 2012. The Dark Shadows Convention is being held in Tarrytown, New York. I attended this convention with a very, very, heavy heart, also with tears mirrored within my eyes; the main Character, Jonathan Frid, who was responsible for Dark Shadows to become a phenomenal success, and influenced the Dark Shadows Convention for being held each year across the vast distance Within the United States, had passed.

This was truly, truly a shock to the fans of the late Jonathan Frid. Many tributes were read to honor the man and his legacy of work within the performing arts. Yes, Jonathan Frid had went to that City of Gold to be with the rest of the cast members from the Original Dark Shadows Serial. As a reminder, Jonathan Frid played the sympathetic vampire Barnabas Collins.

CHAPTER NINE

The Year is 2016. The Dark Shadows Convention is being held In Tarrytown, New York. This convention marked a high two points. The first high point is that this celebration at the Doubletree Hotel in Tarrytown, NY concerning Dark Shadows marked its Fiftieth Anniversary of being in existence as a serial, and also being Remembered and celebrated at the conventions. The program contained a nice section to celebrate the triumph of Dark Shadows still being here for fifty years. It was known as the Anniversary album. The second high point is that I attended this convention with a Master's Degree in Business Communications from the now closed Jones International University.

I attended this convention in high class. I was driven to Tarrytown, New York in a stretch *limousine with a chauffeur.* It was an exciting and worthwhile experience. I hope to attend more Dark Shadows convention(s) in the future. Until next time, until Next flashback, until next parallel world adventure, and regular present Time period, may the bite be with you.

CONCLUSION

In conclusion, Dark shadows Convention was a marvelous meeting Place to cherish, reflect, and look forward to future accomplishments That the Dark Shadows serial inspired since its debut since 1966.

Dark Shadows has inspired movies (about itself), continuous sequels concerning the main plot (Barnabas being a vampire), books, Written by various authors, and DVD's pertaining to its episodes. Truly, Dark Shadows captured the good and evil within Man (Both Male and Female). It explores ways that the two sides may Come together to eliminate evil altogether.

PHOTOGRAPHS

2019/06/14
22:41

2019/06/14
22:41